QUEUE

SPOT THE BOOK TITLE

Drawings and Verses
by Simon Drew

moled wine

ANTIQUE COLLECTORS' CLUB

to
caroline

spot the artist

© 2000 Simon Drew
World copyright reserved

ISBN 978 1 85149 356 2

Reprinted 2003, 2008, 2012

British Library Cataloguing-in-Publication Data
A catalogue record for this book is available from the British Library

FSC
www.fsc.org

MIX
Paper from
responsible sources
FSC® C021256

Published by the Antique Collectors' Club Ltd., Sandy Lane, Old Martlesham, Woodbridge, Suffolk IP12 4SD
Printed and bound in China

iNTRODuCTioN

This is a book for people with twisted brains. Most pages contain cryptic puzzles of the 'SPOT THE' variety. These should not be confused with the pages which have no puzzles but which are designed to be confusing.

On a 'SPOT THE' page you may be presented with a single puzzle or asked to identify several separate items which are indicated by numbered lines.

It is possible to look for hidden meanings on every page. However beware of

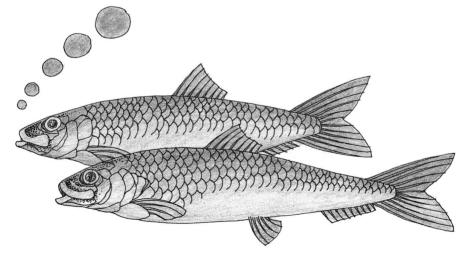

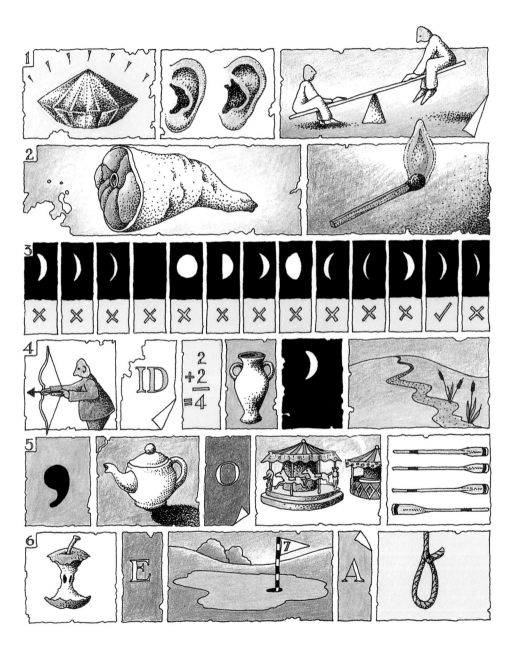

spot the film stars

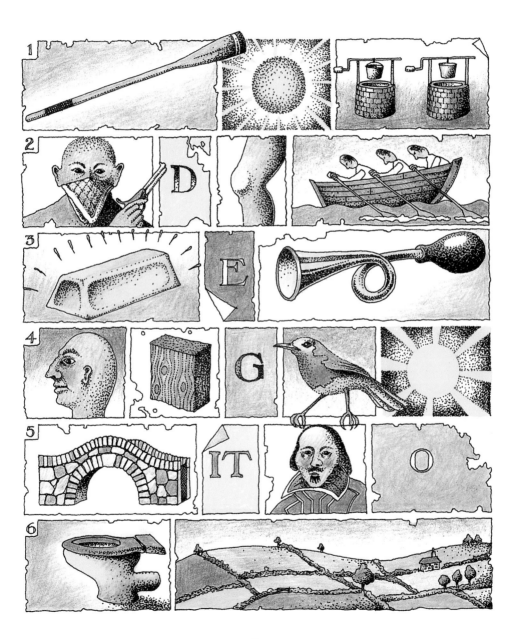

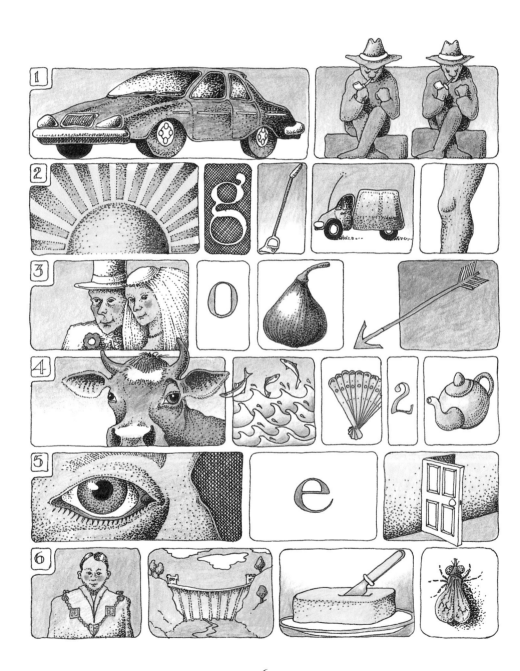

spot the beatles song

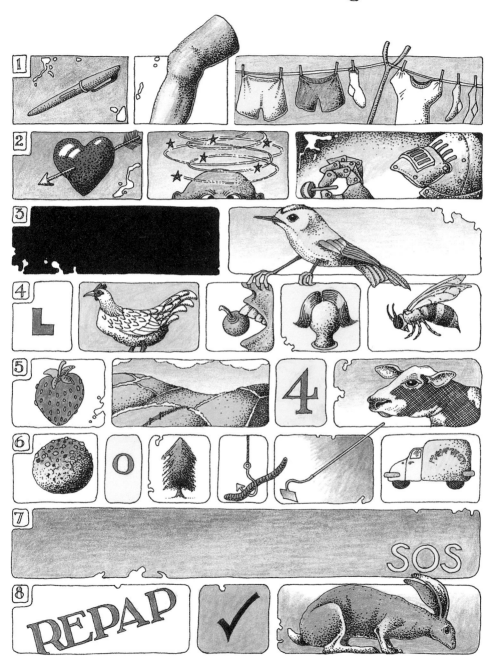

spot the elvis song

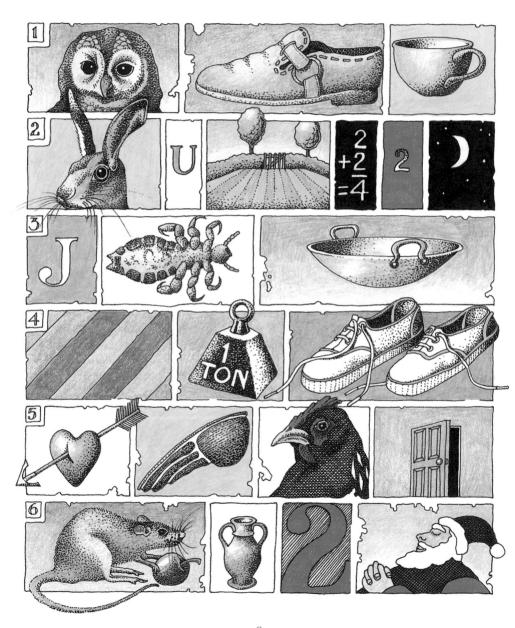

spot the inventor:

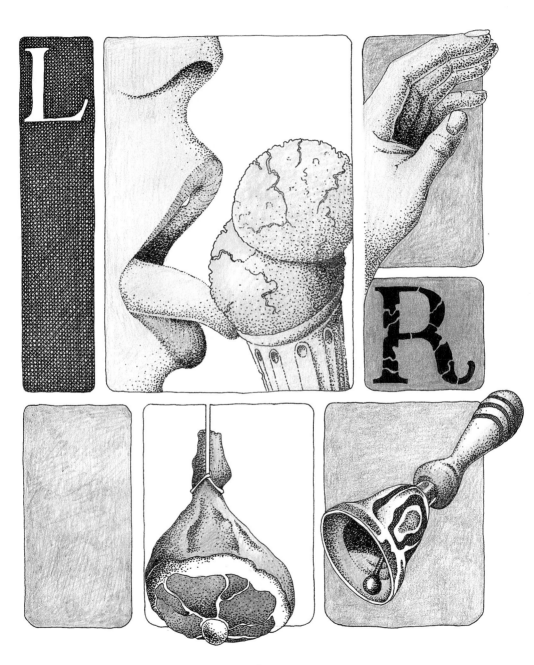

spot the book title

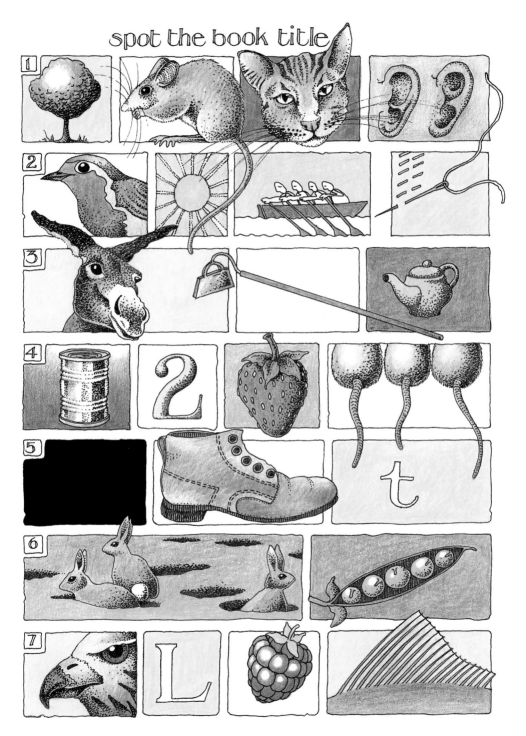

SPOT THE SINGER

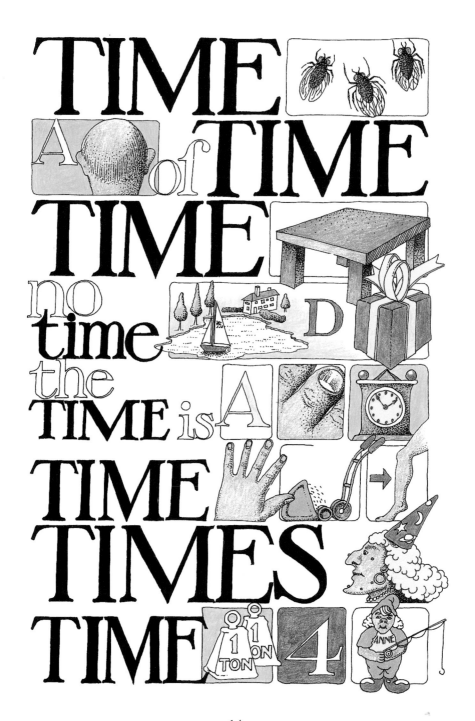

spot the mammal

15

SPOT THE COUNTRY

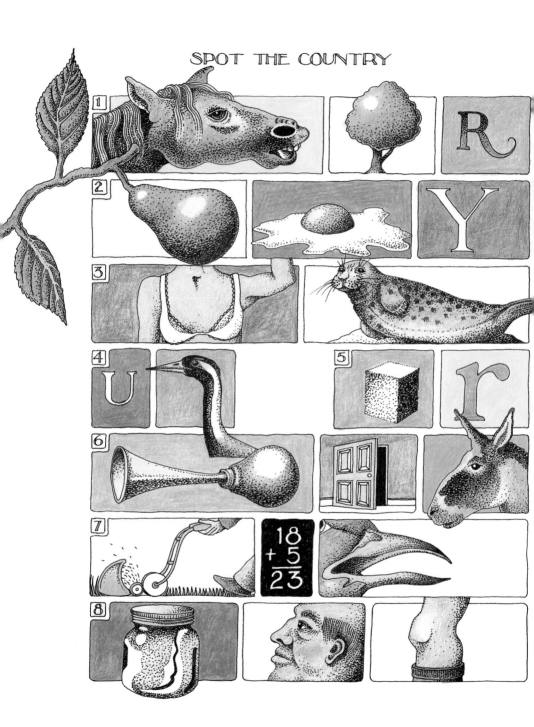

17

spot the car:

spot the american state:

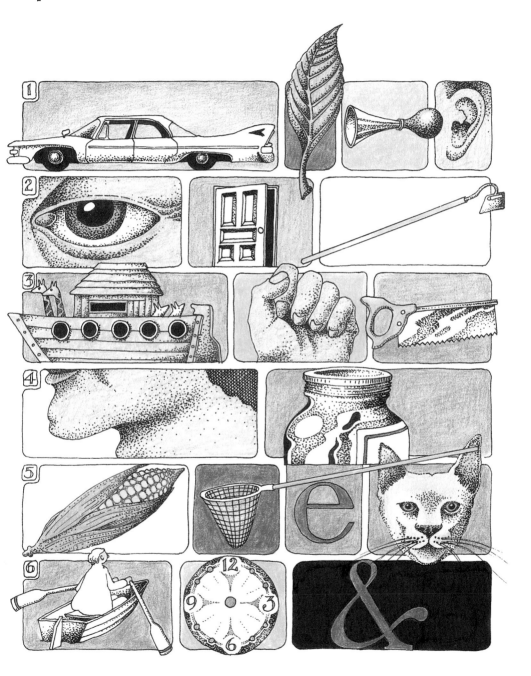

19

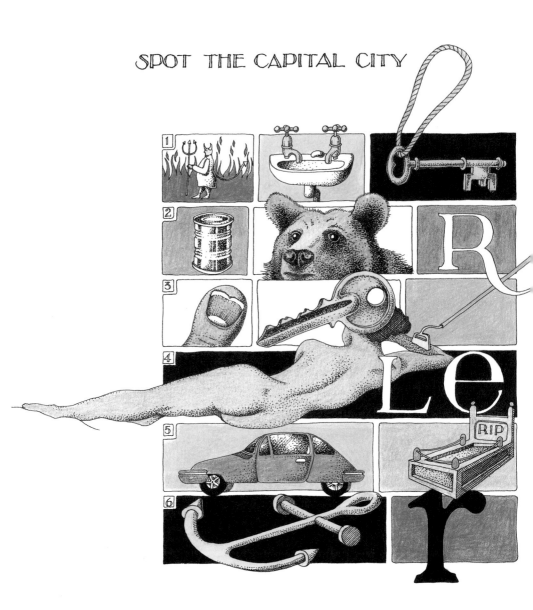

(fractions speak louder than worms)

The Marriage Vows Explained

with this wed

with my bored E I V

with all my 🌍 lee goods

end: 'OW'

spot the bird

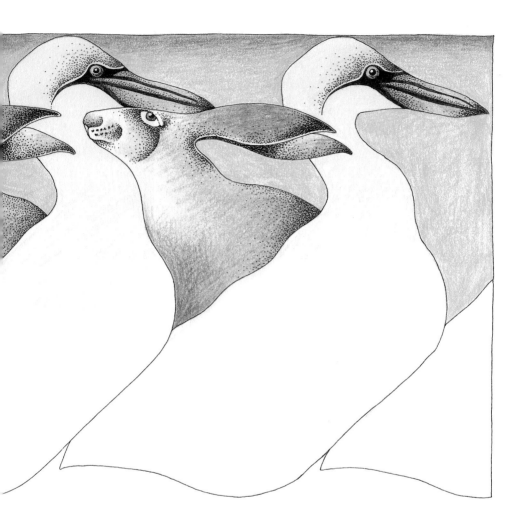

THIS HAPPY BREED

Was human existence well planned
and were we supposed to be free?
When pregnant young women are scanned
and men feed on haddock for tea,
are we breeding like rabbits on land
and eating like gannets at sea?

Question: How many cockerels make a heap?
Answer : 6

Explanation: pile cockerels on top of each
other. Count them from the top: 'Cock one,
cock two....etc'   When you get
to 'cock six' you will know that you
have reached the bottom.

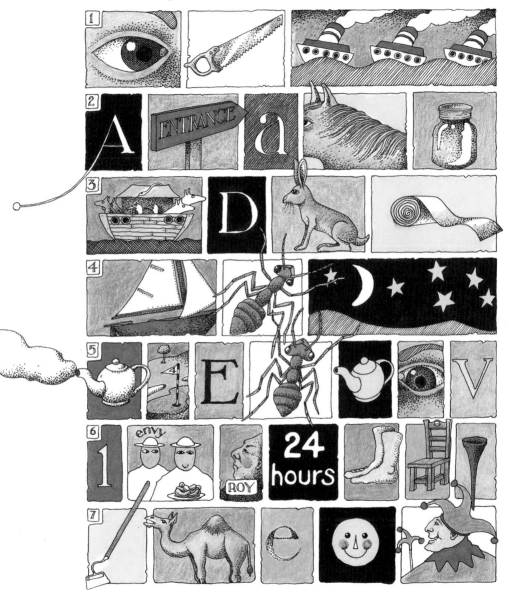

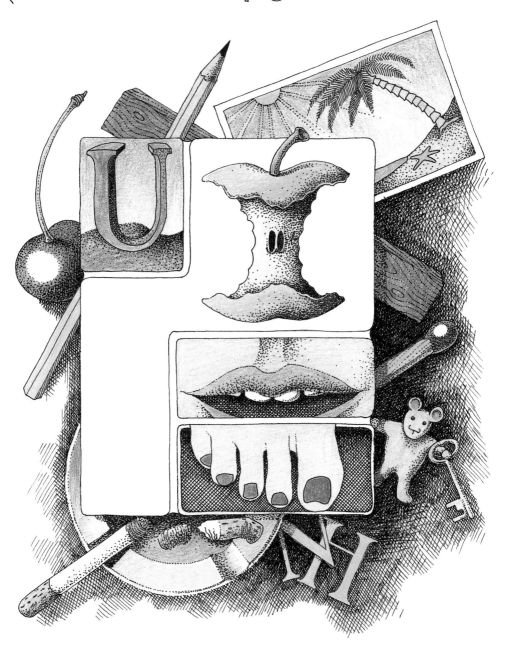

29

30

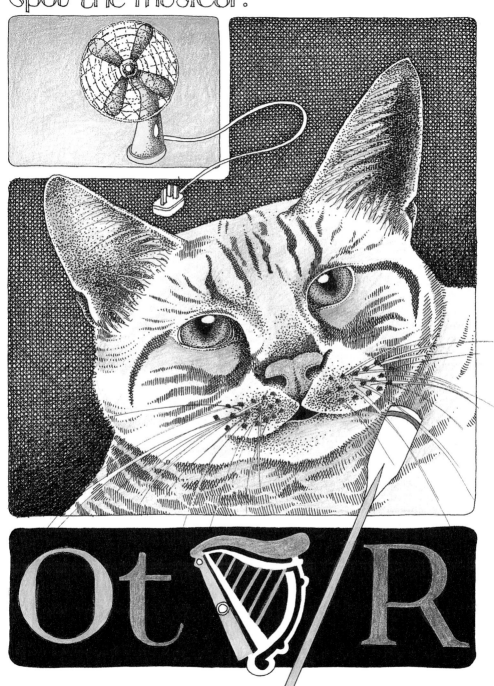

SPOT THE COMPOSER

cities of the world

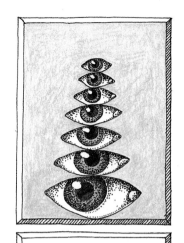

PARIS

(the eye-ful tower)

NEW YORK

(eye skating
in central park)

LONDON

(eyed park)

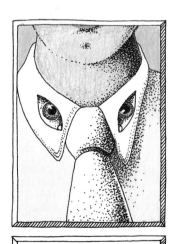

ROME

(the collars see 'em)

spot the historical character:

Ode to a Nightjar

9

The Smiths have a beautiful garden
with a nightjar which nests in their yew
but it comes out and sings around lunchtime
so they call the house Day Jar View.

SPOT THE GILBERT AND SULLIVAN OPERETTA

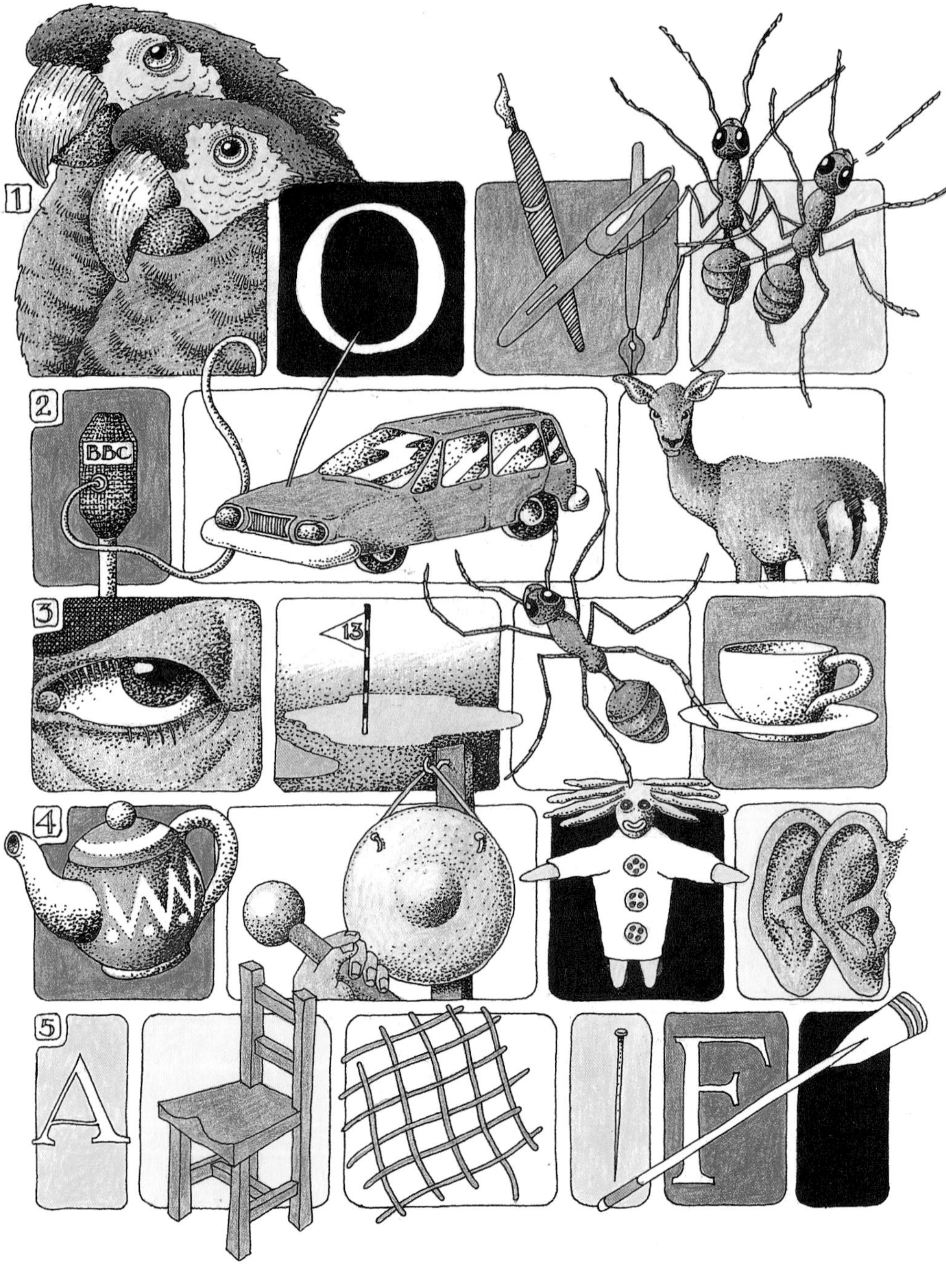

I get no crick from your neck
I know, when sick, I need only one peck
to restore bon homie, and joy too
'cos I get a cork out of you.

spot the shakespeare line

spot the shakespeare line

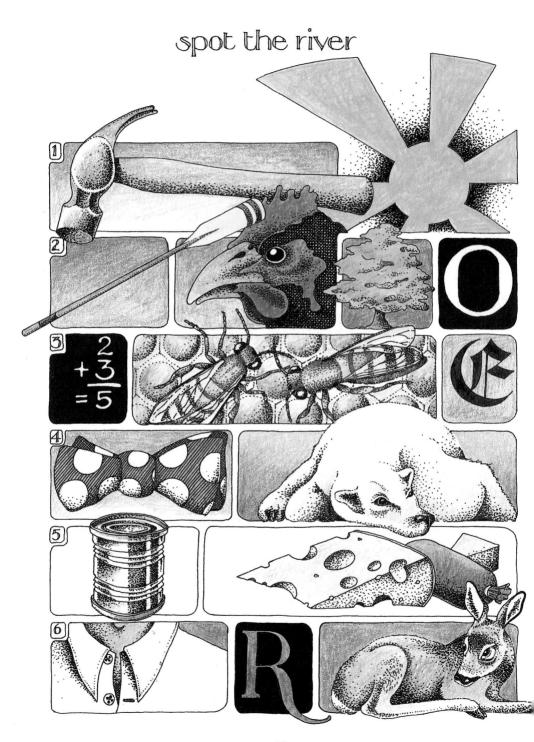

spot the fish

the origins of pasta

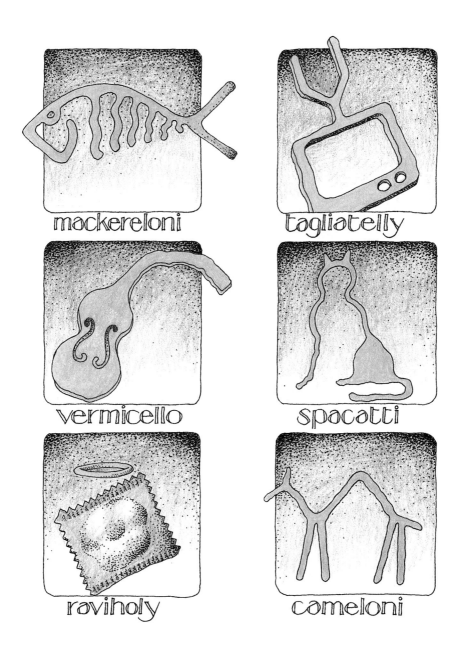

mackereloni

tagliatelly

vermicello

spacatti

raviholy

cameloni

spot the book of the bible

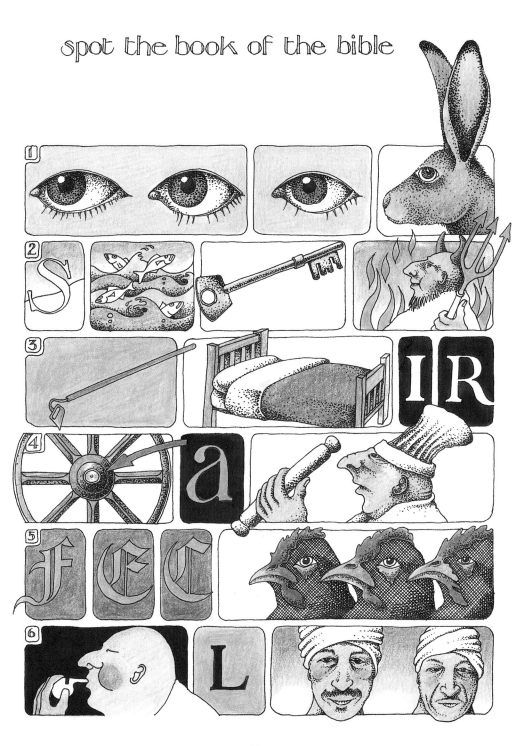

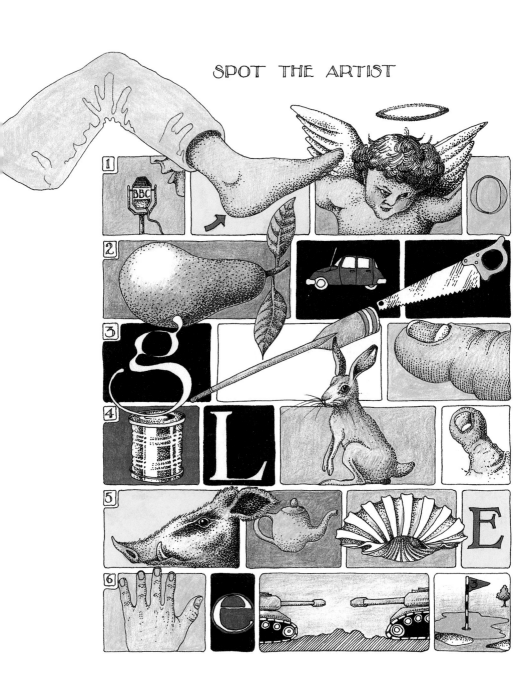

ANSWERS

Some of the pages in this book are not
puzzles. However some pages are, and
answers may be hard to find.   If you
are unable to work out the answers
you may wish to throw this book from
the nearest window. However if you
really want to know the answers and
cannot wait any longer, you will need to
pay.
Write to this address: simon drew
    gallery, foss street, dartmouth,
    devon TQ6 9DR england.
    and enclose a cheque for £5
    made out to friends of the Earth
    or cash for £5 or equivalent
    which will be forwarded to
    Friends of the Earth in London.

This is not a payment: it's a fine
for giving up.

(Postscript: there are at least
10 boys' names and 3 girls' names
on this page).

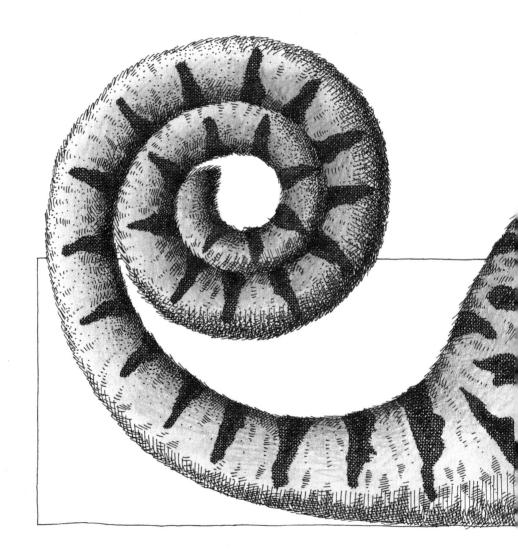